WOHLFAHRT

Studies, Op. 45

Book 1

For Violin
with Newly Composed Violin Accompaniments

Studies 1–30 from 60 Studies, Op. 45

ISBN 978-1-4950-0563-3

ED 4598

G. SCHIRMER, Inc.

DISTRIBUTED BY

HAL•LEONARD®
CORPORATION
7777 W. BLUEMOUND RD. P.O. BOX 13819 MILWAUKEE, WI 53213

www.musicsalesclassical.com
www.halleonard.com

CONTENTS

Studies

Franz Wohlfahrt
Op. 45, Book I

Hold the fingers down as long as possible. Keep the left wrist very quiet.

Articulation and bowing options:

No. 1, Allegro moderato

No. 2, Allegro moderato

In the second etude, the same bowings that
were given for the first etude are to be used.

In the third etude, the same bowings that
were given for the first etude are to be used.

No. 3, Moderato

No. 4, Allegretto

No. 5, Moderato

10

No. 6, Moderato

In the seventh etude, the same bowings that
were given for the first etude are to be used.

No. 7, Allegro moderato

12

No. 8, Largo

Pay attention to G♯ on the D-string and to D on the A-string.

No. 10, Moderato

14

Look out for D on the A-string and for A♭ on the E-string.

No. 11, Moderato

No. 12, Allegro

16

No. 13, Moderato

No. 14, Allegro non tanto

No. 15, Allegro

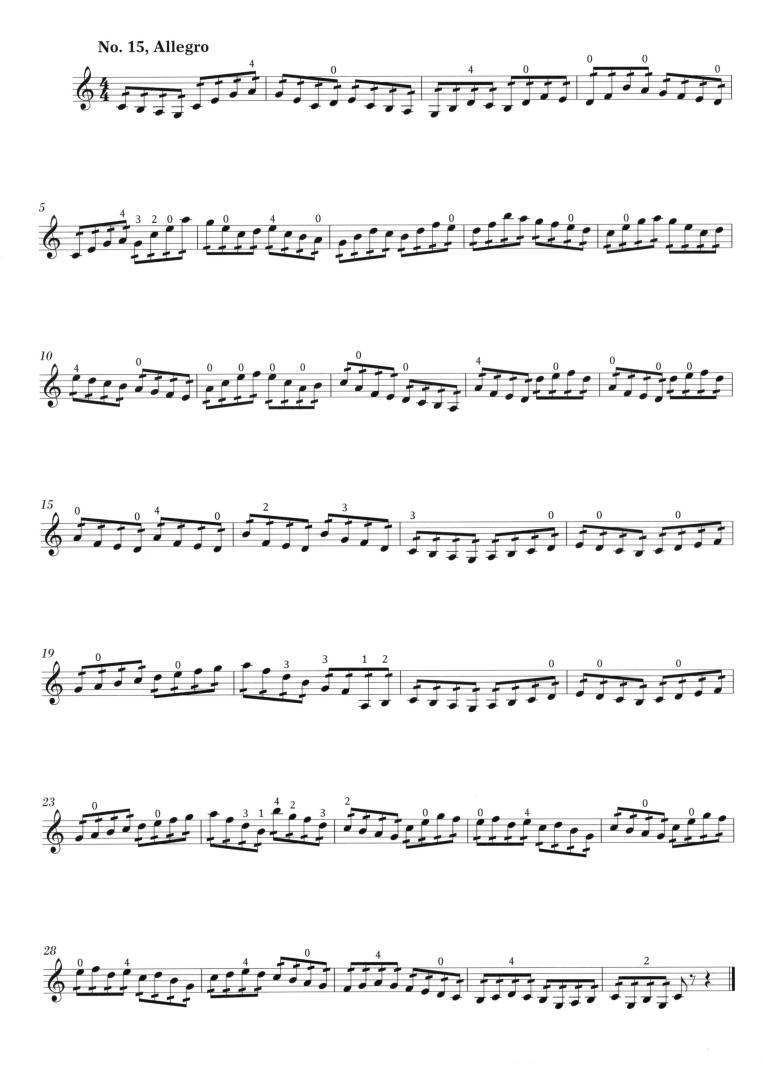

No. 16, Moderato

No. 17, Moderato assai

No. 18, Allegro

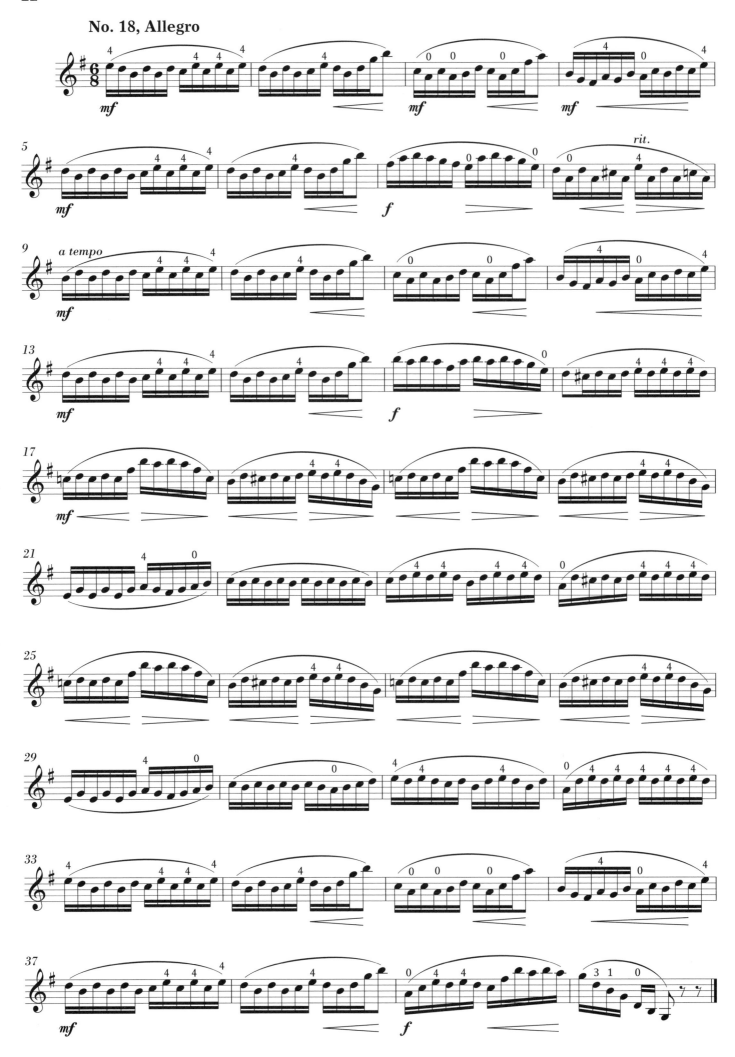

In the last three measures, employ
the same bowing without change.

No. 19, Moderato

24

No. 20, Allegro

Editor's Note: This etude is to be played in simple meter, not with a triplet rhythm.

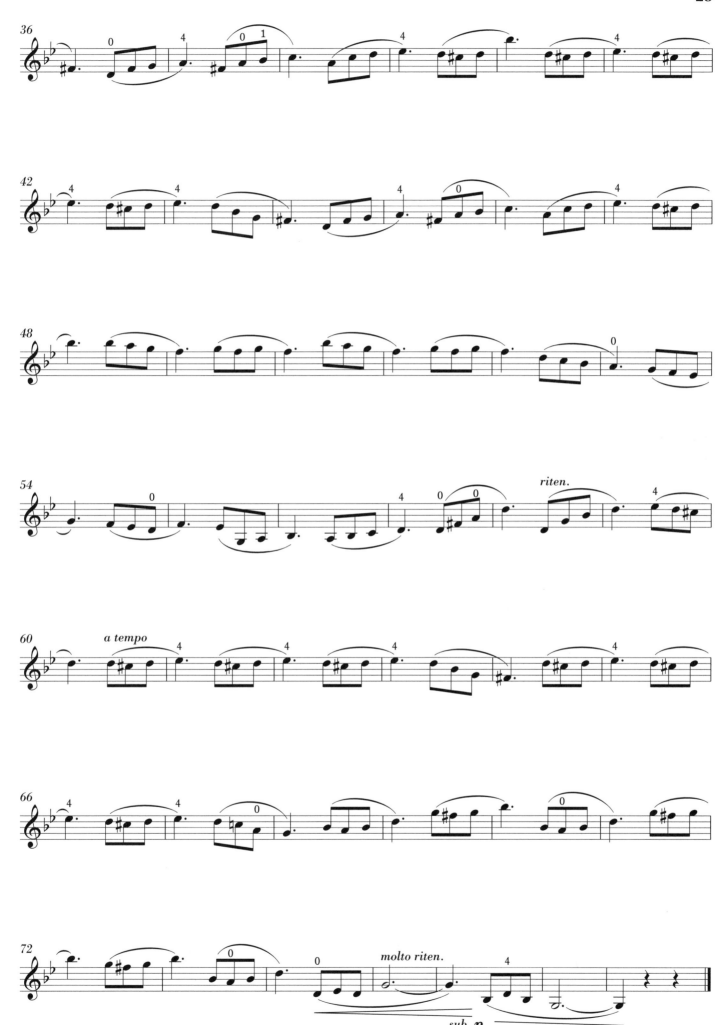

No. 21, Allegro

No. 22, Allegro

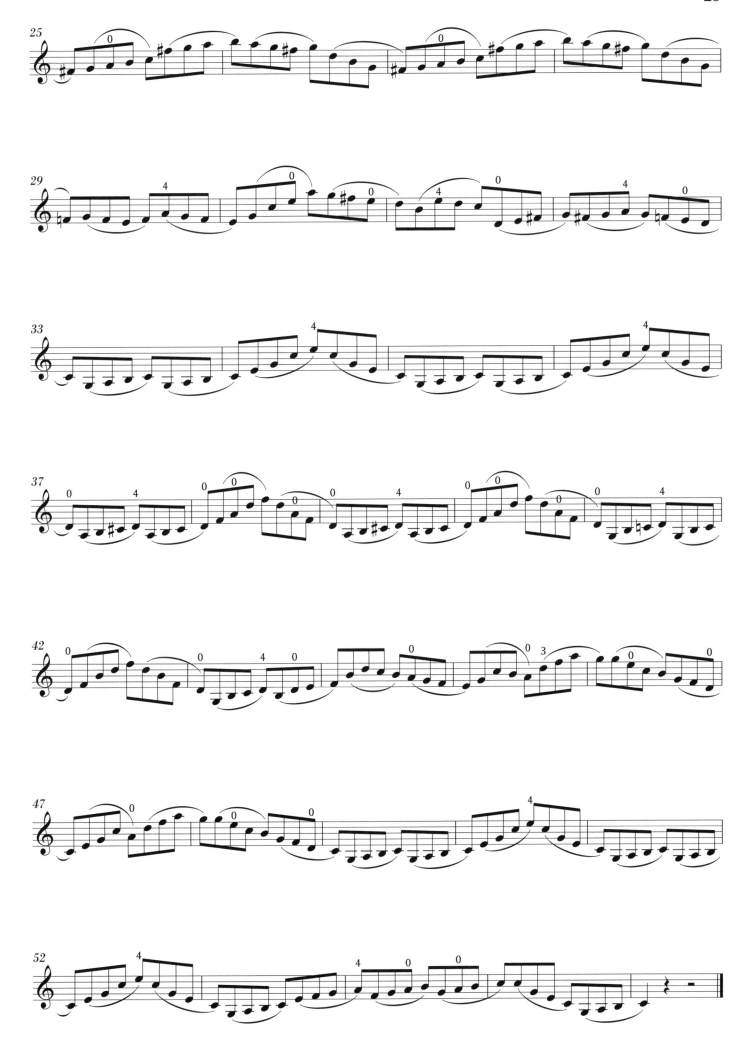

30

No. 23, Moderato

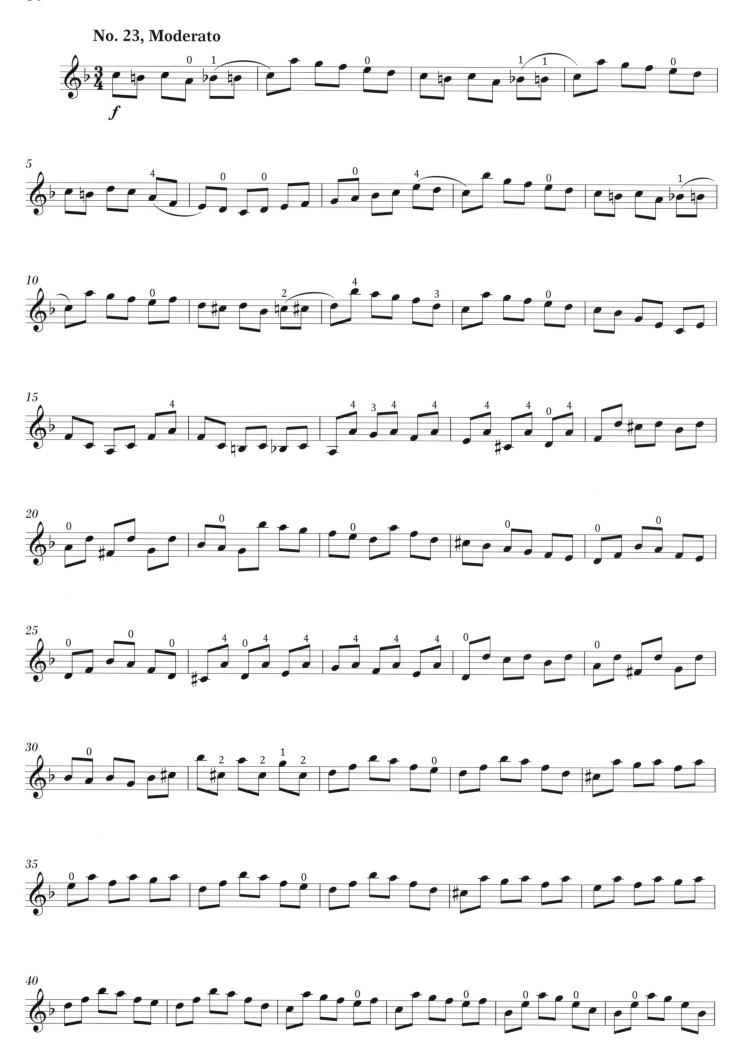

No. 24, Moderato assai

32

No. 25, Allegro

No. 26, Allegro

34

No. 27, Allegro

No. 28, Allegretto

No. 29, Moderato

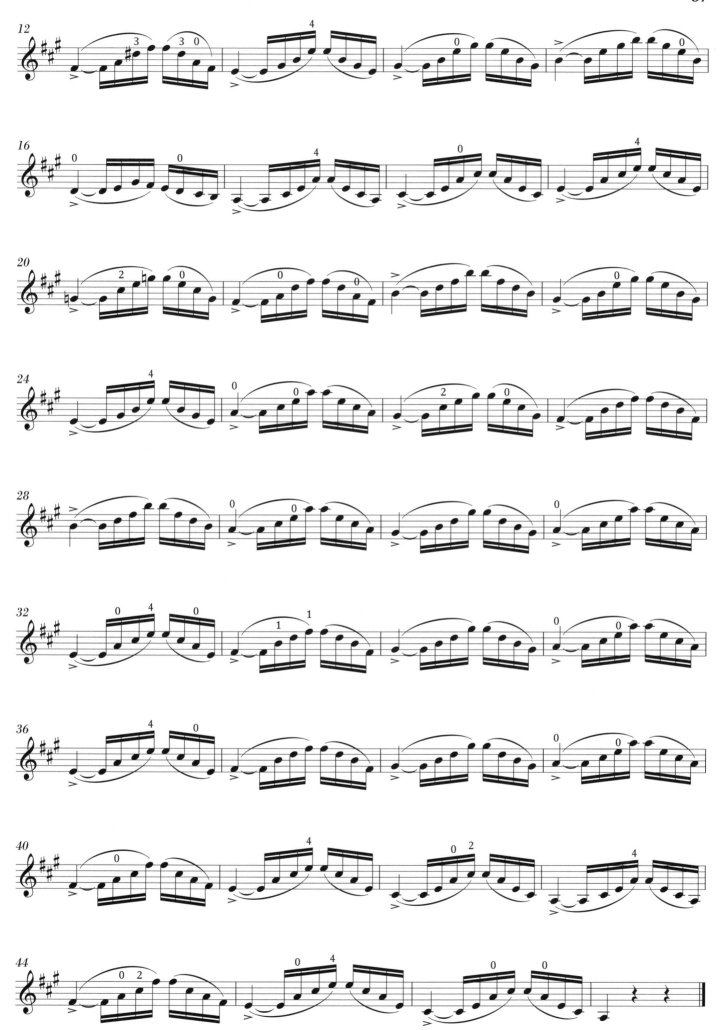

38

No. 30, Allegro

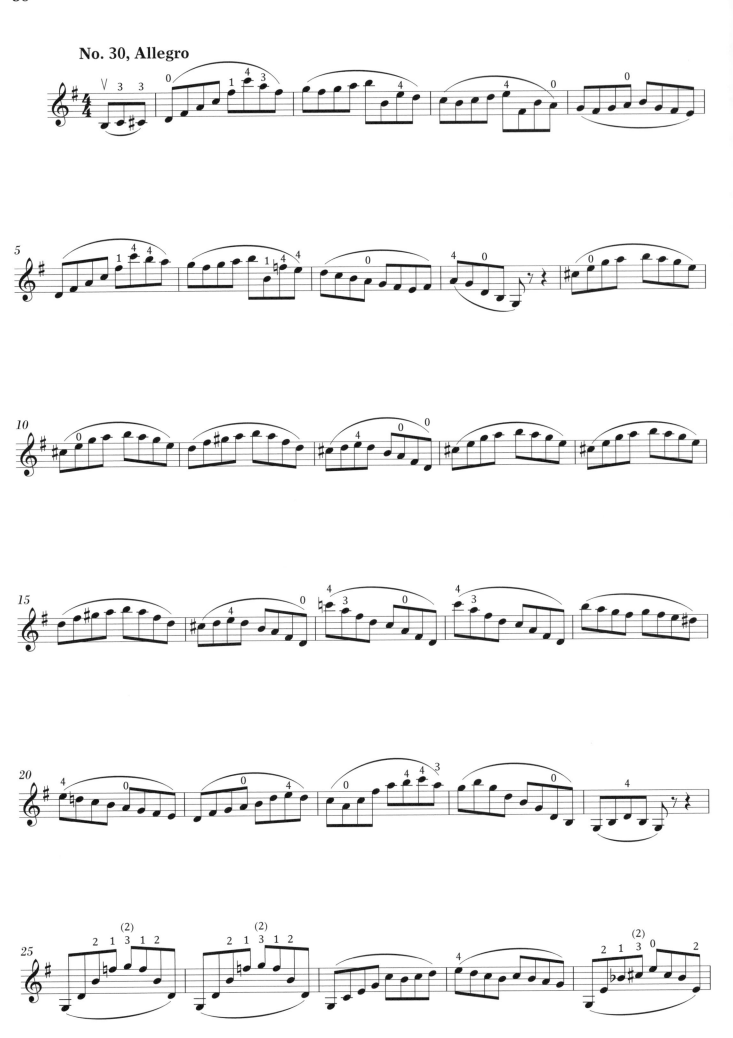